YOUR KNOWLEDGE HAS VALUE

- We will publish your bachelor's and
  master's thesis, essays and papers

- Your own eBook and book -
  sold worldwide in all relevant shops

- Earn money with each sale

Upload your text at www.GRIN.com
and publish for free

John-Robert Funck

Concept of an internet-based operating system

GRIN Publishing

Bibliographic information published by the German National Library:

The German National Library lists this publication in the National Bibliography;
detailed bibliographic data are available on the Internet at http://dnb.dnb.de .

Imprint:

Copyright © 2006 GRIN Verlag GmbH
Print and binding: Books on Demand GmbH, Norderstedt Germany
ISBN: 978-3-656-83556-1

Concept of an Internet-based Operating System

author:

John-Robert Funck

Table of content

1 Introduction

Nowadays data processing is usually done on computers. On these computers it is necessary to have an operating system (OS) installed which manages the relationship between application software and hardware managing tasks. This kind of system has worked well so far.

However, there are various problems with a built-in operating system. It requires powerful and expensive hardware to operate smoothly. Additionally complex operation knowledge is necessary and often there are compatibility issues among programs. Moreover there is a waste of time due to maintenance and so forth.

My solution to the problems mentioned above is an internet-based operating system. In this paper I will describe a way to improve data processing while getting rid of the built-in operating system and its shortcomings. At first I will explain the underlying structure of my solution and in the next part I will suggest how this structure can be realized. Afterwards I will discuss the advantages and disadvantages of my solution and finally I will give a brief overview of current developments of internet-based operating systems.

2 Internet-based Operating System

Operating systems are more than just a piece of program code. They are written with specific hardware and software in mind so one has to consider these things while developing it.

An internet-based operating system should be based on the client-server principle [1]. Each instance of the client can send requests to the server where the operating system resides. Requests will be sent over the internet to the remote server and will be processed as requested. In the following paragraphs I will explain in detail which hardware and which software is required on the client and on the server side.

2.1 Hardware requirements

Generally the hardware required does not differ very much from today's hardware. In fact everything can be done on available hardware.

2.1.1 Hardware on the client side

Thin clients are widely used today therefore they can be used for the hardware basis on the client side. The very thin client should consist of a monitor with integrated interfaces for all the periphery such as a scanner, the keyboard or a printer. Additionally high speed wired and wireless network should be built-in to connect to the internet everywhere and to upload and receive data. With this solution a powerful CPU and other expensive hardware becomes redundant because the monitor just submits data and receives a video signal. On top of that, with the lack of these components the chance of a system crash will decrease significantly.

The development of the client is a fairly easy task because similar hardware is already available, a bit more complicated will be the development of the server hardware.

2.1.2 Hardware on the server side

Due to the expected traffic and workload the requirements for the server are very high. To compensate this workload a super computer build as a cluster is required. Clustering can provide significant performance benefits versus price (almost every super computer today is build as a cluster [2]).

Another main advantage of the cluster is the modular installation where hardware can be easily extended. It is impossible to give concrete numbers about processing power, storage volume or RAM (Randown Access Memory) yet because it depends on the number of connected clients and their workload demanded. To store all the user data a huge storage volume is needed, therefore it must be made easy to extend it as well. Besides the huge storage volume, lots of Random Access Memory is required to handle the big amount of data processing.

Below is a picture to illustrate the interaction of the client and server:

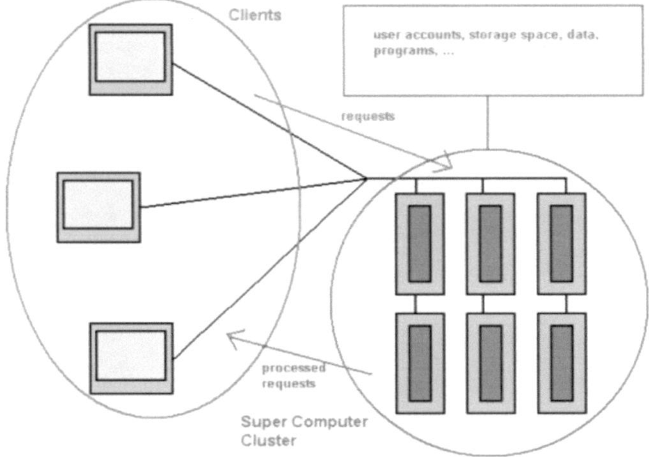

Figure 1: Interaction between client and server

2.2 Software requirements

Development and implementation of the software remains the main obstacle of the system.

This is the part which requires a lot of work. Writing an operating system takes much time, Mircosoft for instance needs more than 3 years to come up with a new one [3]. Considering that this approach is different than the operating mode of nowadays operating systems it will also be a time consuming task.

2.2.1 Software on the client side

A lean and simple user interface is the most important thing to a computer user. Wroblewski and Rantanen [4] conclude in their paper "Design Considerations for Web-based Applications" that the user should not need to know whether they are interacting with an application over the internet or on their home computer. Users expect a cohesive, elegant, and intuitive user experience which leads to use of the KISS [5] principle while developing it. Only basic software which handles the input of the peripherals and manages the connection to the server is necessary.

The following self-made picture illustrate how a lean and simple user interface could look like:

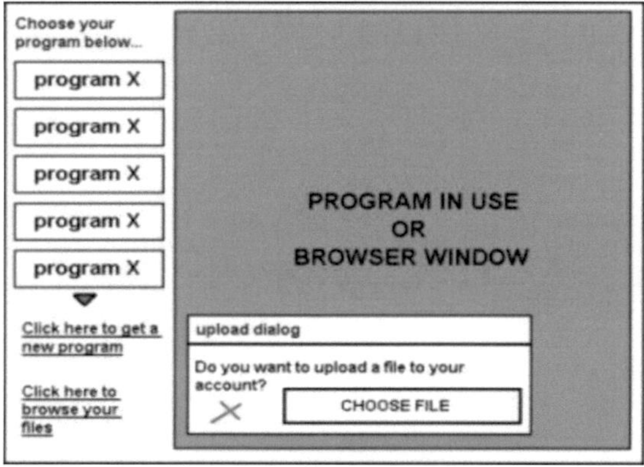

Figure 2: User Interface example

All the background tasks are handled by the remote operating system which will be described in the next part.

2.2.2 *Software on the server side*

Here lies the heart of the operating system. The software on the server side handles all the incoming commands and sends the results back to the client. It also manages the coordination of the computers and software.

In the past Unix (like) operating systems have been proven to be flexible and scalable. Important web pages with huge workload like Google or Wikipedia for instance are based on Unix (like) operating systems. As a conclusion the operating system should be based on Unix.

Every user should be provided with his/her personal account. Depending on a fee, the user is granted with a certain amount of storage and processing capacity. Software companies should be able to install their software on the operating system. In order to use a certain program the user has to pay an additional fee. Installation and maintenance of software becomes redundant for the user because it is done on the server. Security should be another big topic when developing an internet OS. Encrypted connections like the secure socket shell and security systems with a minimum of privileges for the users should ensure the privacy of the user and prevent data theft. Again the user has not be aware of keeping his system save anymore because he/she does not need to install security related programs.

Now that the basic idea of the operating system is discussed we have to take a look at the advantages and disadvantages of an internet-based operating system.

2.3 Advantages and disadvantages of an Internet-based OS

In the following paragraphs I will list the advantages and disadvantages of an internet-based operating system. Of course there are more but I will limit them to the most important ones.

2.3.1 Advantages

Accessibility: Accessibility is one of the main advantages of the operating system. It is possible to use other clients anywhere because all of the data and programs are stored at one's user account on the central server.

Flexibility: Flexibility is another strong point of the operating system. If one needs to use a specific program fast, one just has to order it on one's account and it will be available to him/her instantly. There is no need to install it or going out and buy it anymore.

Ease of use: If one does not have to worry anymore how to install a certain program, how to maintain one's system, how to keep one's system save or how to do a backup of one's files, one will save much time and therefore raise productivity.

Low hardware requirements (on the client side): Due to the simple buildup of the client one does not need expensive hardware anymore. It will be easy to equip a whole company with clients which will save a huge amount of money. Maintenance will also decrease because of less complex hardware.

2.3.2 Disadvantages

Interruption of the connection: One of the major problems is the interruption of the connection. One can not do anything if the connection gets down and it will cause a huge impact if one's work has to be done quick and is from importance. The cause of the interruption could possibly be that one's internet service provider has serious problems or one could have a client hardware crash.

Abuse of one's account: Another main problem is the abuse of the user account. Somebody with mischievous thoughts could shut it down, delete files or copy sensitive information. If IT is a critical success factor, then one will lose his entire business.

The data has to be mirrored (on the server side): It is necessary to do an expensive backup or else the data will get lost. If the operating system servers are run in Los Angeles when the next big earthquake hits or New Orleans during the next big hurricane, your clients become useless boxes. Again, if IT is a critical success factor, one will lose his business.

Privacy issues: For some companies and for most of the home users privacy is a big issue. One can imagine that most of them would not feel very comfortable when knowing that all their critical data is stored in one place.

Speed issues: Yet another week point could be the internet connection speed. Sometimes one needs to upload or download big files, this could probably take some time depending on the connection.

2.4   **Future prospects**

In this section I want to give a brief overview of future prospects of internet-based operating systems.

2.4.1   *General prospects*

The internet will keep on growing because of the increasing number of people who get access to the internet therefore internet-based applications will keep on growing too.

Not only internet-based applications will increase, research on internet-based operating systems is also done by some companies. Below I will present Google's and Ajax's approaches on internet-based operating systems.

2.4.2   *Google OS*

According to Rich Skrenta [6] the well-known search engine giant Google is building a huge computer with a custom operating system that everyone on earth can have an account on.

While competitors are targeting the individual applications Google has deployed, Google is building a massive, general purpose computing platform for web-scale programming.

By building and then joining small internet applications, Google can take full advantage of the economies of scale.

Unfortunately not many information have been released yet because it is still in development but this small approach seems to be very similar to what I have been aiming at.

More concrete information about an internet-based operating system is found for the Ajax OS, which will be described below.

2.4.3   *Ajax OS*

Like Google OS, Ajax OS is a internet-based operating system which is still in development. It has new features to support the adoption of web-based software. Features include: Automatic launch of Ajax software when clicking on a supported file type, the ability to save files to a virtual storage and the ability to navigate through a file browser to the files uploaded to the virtual storage as well those on your local computer. According to Ajax the operating system will have the following advantages which are very similar to the advantages of my approach:

„Information Security - Your files and documents are safe from computer crashes, laptop theft, viruses and other virtual attacks on your computer since they are all saved on ajaxOS remote storage.

Web-based Software Applications Included – Save money. No need to purchase expensive software – it's all included in ajaxOS.

Updated and Upgraded Automatically – Spending time and money on software updates and upgrades is also a thing of the past, most ajaxOS applications are upgraded automatically.

Full file compatibility – applications are compatible with all standard file formats, allowing you to easily transfer your existing files and share files created using AJAX software with others." [7]

3 Conclusion

In summary, developing an internet-based operating system should be possible with nowadays hardware. As mentioned previously the most work has to been done in the software department. Although there are disadvantages the main advantages of an internet-based operating system is the accessibility and the flexibility which can not be achieved with solutions of today. These strong points contain great potential. It will be challenging to realize the structure of an internet-based operating system but as soon as we have overcome this obstacle the way is free for enhanced data processing.

Postscript

The inspiration for this paper came from my interest for internet-based applications and operating systems. I often experienced the shortcomings of operating systems and wondered why nobody has combined the benefits of the internet with an operating system to overcome these shortcomings. This was the point for thinking about how an internet-based operating system could look like and how it works.

References

[1]   R. Orfali, D. Harkey, J. Edwards, *Essential Client/Server Survival Guide*, John Wiley & Sons; New Ed edition, June 1994

[2]   A. J. van der Steen and J. J. Dongarra, *Overview of Recent Supercomputers*, Report from   March 7, 2005 , http://www.top500.org/orsc/2005/

[3]   Microsoft, *Windows Products and Technologies History*, June 30, 2003, http://www.microsoft.com/windows/WinHistoryIntro.mspx

[4]   L. Wroblewski and E. M. Rantanen, *Design Considerations for Web-based Applications*, Human Factors and Ergonomics Society's Annual Meeting, 2001, http://www.lukew.com/resources/articles/web_applications.html

[5]   E. S. Raymond, *The New Hacker's Dictionary*, The MIT Press, 1996, http://www.outpost9.com/reference/jargon/jargon_toc.html

[6]   J. Kottke, *GooOS, the Google Operating System*, April 06, 2004, http://www.kottke.org/04/04/google-operating-system

[7]   Ajax 13, *the AJAX aware operating system*, 2006, http://www.myajaxos.com/